Creative Crafts
for kids

Paper Crafts
With Pizzazz

Tracy Nelson Maurer

ROURKE PUBLISHING

Vero Beach, Florida 32964

www.rourkepublishing.com

Author Acknowledgments
Thank you to Meg and Tommy, Mike, Adrian, and to the crews at Rourke and Blue Door.

Photo credits: All photos © Blue Door Publishing except: Title Page © Leo Blanchette, vectorstock, RLN; Contents Page © CABO; Page 4 © Tania Zbrodko, Lynn Watson; Page 5 © Heidi Brand, Lemony; Page 6 © Graham S. Klotz; Page 7 © Elena Schweitzer; Page 21 © Petronilo G. Dangoy Jr.; Page 30 © Jean L F

Editor: Meg Greve

Cover and page design by Nicola Stratford, Blue Door Publishing

Library of Congress Cataloging-in-Publication Data

Maurer, Tracy, 1965-
  Paper crafts with pizzazz : creative crafts for kids / Tracy Nelson Maurer.
     p. cm. -- (Creative crafts for kids)
  Includes index.
  ISBN 978-1-60694-342-7 (hard cover)
  ISBN 978-1-60694-504-9 (soft cover)
  1. Paper work--Juvenile literature. I. Title.
TT870.M383 2009
745.592--dc22
                                   2009003895

Printed in the USA

ROURKE PUBLISHING

www.rourkepublishing.com - rourke@rourkepublishing.com
Post Office Box 643328 Vero Beach, Florida 32964

contents

A World of Paper

People around the world have made paper for thousands of years. Ancient Egyptians used the **papyrus** plant to make a writing paper. The word for paper comes from papyrus.

The Chinese and Japanese created thin papers from rice plants. In A.D. 105, Ts'ai Lun of China invented paper from mulberry bark and rags. Later, Aztecs and Mayans boiled bark from wild mulberry and fig trees to make a rough paper called *amatl*.

Before the 1600s, European leaders mainly used thin parchment made from animal skins for written works.

4

People used stalks of the papyrus plant to make the first paper.

Even today, cotton fibers create strong and durable paper.

Most paper is still made with fibers from trees or cotton plants, including fibers **recycled** from used paper.

Recycle Your Used Paper

Do you recycle paper products? Recycling paper saves trees, uses less water and energy, and keeps garbage out of landfills.

What is made from recycled paper? Here are just a few products.

- writing and printing paper
- food boxes
- tissues and paper towels
- garden mulch and compost
- packaging
- kitty litter
- construction materials

Paper Works of Art

In every ancient culture that has made paper, the leaders prized the handmade material. The Aztecs even used it like money. Over time, artists in each ancient culture used paper for drawing, painting, writing, folding, cutting, or sculpting. Paper artists today use many of the same **techniques** that ancient artists used.

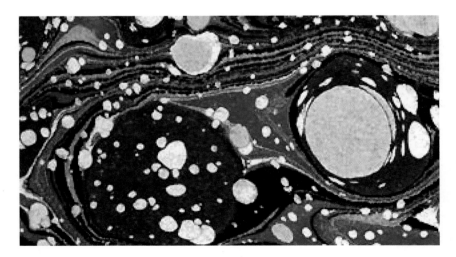

Colorful marbled papers were made centuries ago in Central Asia and in the Middle East.

Unlike artists of the past, you can find affordable paper in many colors, textures, and weights just about anywhere. Look in discount stores, art supply shops, or online.

Get Ready!

Gather these supplies in a box or bucket to keep them handy for your projects.

- pencil
- craft or tacky glue
- scissors
- ruler with a metal edge
- pencil
- markers or crayons

You Will Need:

- 1 sheet of white copy paper or colored construction paper 8-1/2 x 11 inches (21.5 x 28 centimeters)
- scissors
- markers or colored pencils
- pen or pencil

8

Amaze your friends with your ability to tell their fortunes. Just follow these simple steps to see into the future!

Here's How:

1. Turn the paper so that it is wider rather than longer. Fold the bottom left corner up to the long side, matching the edges. Cut off the extra strip, so that you have a triangle.

2. Fold the triangle in half again, so that you have a smaller triangle.

3. Open your paper all the way. The folds should look like an x.

4. Turn the paper so it looks like a diamond. Take one corner and fold it up to the center point of the square.

5. Repeat folding with each corner until you have a small square.

6. Turn the square over so that you are looking at the smooth side without folds.

7. Turn the square so it looks like a diamond. Take one corner and fold it up to the center point of the square.

8. Repeat folding with the other three corners until you have a smaller square.

9. Now you can decorate your fortune-teller. Open the square up again. In the tops of the triangles, write a fortune such as, *You will get an A on your test today* or *If you bake cookies, you will have many friends.*

10. Fold the square back up with the points facing in. Each of the triangles should have two sections. On each of those sections, write a number in the center. Think of the outside of the square as the top of each triangle.

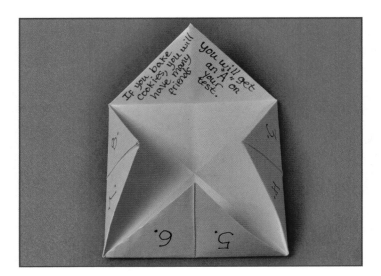

11. Fold the points back in and turn the square over. You should have four smaller squares on the other side. Make a different color dot or star on each square.

12. Turn the square back over. Fold the square in half to make a rectangle. Fold it in half again to make a much smaller square. Press on the creases.

13. Open the square again. With the colored dots side up, push the four points together while tucking your fingers into the flaps under the squares. You should be able to open and close your fortune-teller.

T i P

Instead of writing numbers, you can challenge your friends by writing a math problem.

To Tell Fortunes:

1. Put your fingers in your fortune-teller without opening it.

2. Ask your friend to pick a color. Open and close your fortune-teller while spelling the color. For example, if your friend chooses red, open and close your fortune-teller three times. Leave it open on the last letter.

3. Ask your friend to choose a number. Open and close your fortune-teller that number of times.

4. Open your fortune-teller and ask your friend to choose another number.

5. Open that flap and reveal your friend's fortune.

You Will Need:

- 1 sheet of craft foam
- scissors
- fabric glue
- 3 x 3 inch (7.5 x 7.5 centimeter) wooden blocks
- poster paint in a low, flat dish or stamp pads
- white or colored paper with matching envelopes
- copy paper
- pencil
- marker with thin tip

Create your own stationery or make writing paper sets to give to your friends. Use one design or several designs.

Here's How:

1. Draw a design on paper, such as a heart, star, or flower. Or make a pattern, such as a set of dots. Your design should be smaller than a 3 x 3 inch (7.5 x 7.5 centimeter) square.

2. Cut out the design.

3. Trace the paper design onto the craft foam and cut it out.

4. Glue the craft foam to the wooden block. Let it dry.

5. Load the stamp with color by pressing it on the pad or dipping it in paint; press the image onto a corner of the paper, or wherever you like. Load the stamp again and press a matching image on an envelope.

6. Add details to your design with a marker.

For small circles, such as flower centers, dip the eraser end of a pencil in paint and use as a stamp.

You Will Need:

- 2 pieces of card stock in two colors
- craft glue
- scissors
- markers or crayons

TIP

If you have trouble making the mouth pop up, fold your creases again in the opposite direction. Gently poke the triangles through to the inside of the card and fold them into place.

Pop-up Birthday Card

I HOPE YOUR BIRTHDAY ROARS!

This fun card surprises your friends. Make several cards with different faces, such as a duck, a frog, a bird, or any wild creature that you imagine.

Here's How:

1. Make the inside first. Turn the lighter piece of paper horizontally and fold it in half. Cut a slit about 2 inches (5 centimeters) through the fold, halfway between the top and bottom edges.

2. Fold back each cut edge to make a triangle on each side. Snip tiny angles out of the slit edges for teeth.

3. Open the card and pinch the point of each triangle.

4. Close the card, guiding the triangles to fold inside. The creased edge should now look like a triangle is missing from it.

5. Open the card. Draw a big circle around the cut for the face. Draw round eyes inside the circle. Color in the face. Write a message such as, *I hope your birthday roars!*

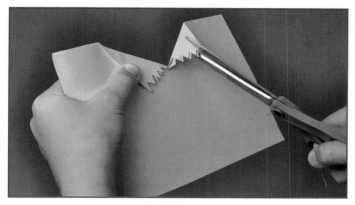

6. To create the outside, fold the darker piece of paper in half.

7. Glue the dark paper to the outside of the mouth card. Do not glue the mouth or the card will not open.

- 2 pieces of 8-1/2 x 11 inch (21.5 x 28 centimeter) card stock, in two colors
- craft glue
- scissors
- markers or crayons
- printed picture of you

Picture Frame Thank You Card

Say thank you with a picture that shows how much you like your gift. Ask a parent to take a digital picture of you and print it from the computer to fit a 5 x 7 inch (12.5 x 17.5 centimeter) card for your special project.

Here's How:

1. To make the outside frame, measure 5-1/2 inches (14 centimeters) on the widest sides of the darker paper. Draw a line and cut the paper in halves. Save the extra half for another project.

2. Fold the darker paper in half so the two longest edges meet. Trim the paper edges. Do not cut the fold. Make the trim wavy or any pattern you like.

3. With the frame still folded, move in about 1 inch (2.5 centimeters) from the side. Cut through the fold toward the open edge opposite of the fold. Stop about 1 inch (2.5 centimeters) from the open edge. Continue cutting until you make a border about 1 inch (2.5 centimeters) wide all the way around.

4. Place the frame over your photo. Trim the photo if it is too large.

5. Put glue on the front edges of the photo and attach your picture so it faces out of the front of the frame.

6. Put glue on the back of the dark paper frame. Glue it to the outside front of the light card.

7. Write your thank you note on the inside of the card.

What Should You Say?

Send a thank you note for a gift as soon as you can. But it is never too late! Here is a sample to help you start your note. Fill in the blanks to personalize your message.

Dear (*Your Friend's Name*),

Thank you for the nice
_____.

I like it because _____.

Sincerely,

(*Your name*)

You Will Need:

- 1 cup (99 grams) all-purpose white flour
- 1 tablespoon (15 grams) salt
- 1 cup (237 milliliters) water for the glue
- extra water
- newspaper
- 2 large bowls
- sharp pencil or toothpick
- wax paper
- craft paint
- paintbrush
- glitter glue and markers
- craft sealer paint
- 24 inches (61 centimeters) string, yarn, cord, or ribbon

Papier-mâché Beads

Papier-mâché is a French word meaning chewed-up paper, because of how the **pulp** looks. Everywhere in the world, artists have created glued paper structures. Start with small beads. Then work up to larger sculptures.

Here's How:

make The Glue

1. Mix the flour and salt in a large mixing bowl.

2. Slowly add the water. Stir the mixture for five minutes. It will look like lumpy cream.

3. Leftover glue will keep for about a week in the refrigerator.

This is a messy project! Wear old clothes, spread plastic over your work surface, and clean up afterward. Be sure to ask for permission before starting this project.

Make the Beads

1. Tear or cut the newspaper into strips, each about 1 x 5 inches (2.5 x 12.7 centimeters). Make at least 3 big handfuls of shredded newspaper. Place in a bowl.

2. Cover the newspaper strips with water and soak for about four hours.

3. Drain the strips and squeeze out as much water as you can.

4. Mix the newspaper with most of the glue. **Knead** the pulp until it is smooth and holds its shape like clay. If it is too soupy, add more newspaper. If it is too dry, dribble more glue and mix again.

5. Shape small balls, about 2 inches (5 centimeters) around. Gently squeeze out extra water as you roll each ball in your hands.

6. Poke a pencil or toothpick through the center of each ball.

7. Let the balls dry for at least two days.

8. Paint the balls with stripes, stars, hearts, and other designs. For extra sparkle, decorate with glitter glue. Let the beads dry for 24 hours.

9. Cover each bead with craft sealer and let dry.

10. Thread the string through the holes in the beads. Then tie the ends in a knot for your necklace.

Layered Art

Another papier-mâché method uses layers of newspaper strips dipped in glue and placed over a form, such as a balloon or wire frame. Most papier-mâché sculptures need at least five layers. **Piñatas** are often made this way.

In the Philippines, traditional red toy ponies are made from papier-mâché.

- lightweight paper, such as copy paper
- ruler
- scissors

Origami Display Box

TIP

Use patterned wrapping paper to make pretty boxes you can match to your room.

Folded paper artwork called **origami** began in ancient China. In the 1100s, the Japanese made even more complex designs, such as animals, useful objects, and artwork. Make this origami display box for your dresser or desk.

Here's How:

1. Cut your paper to a square, at least 4 x 4 inches (10 x 10 centimeters).

2. Fold the square in half. Open the fold. Fold the square in half again the other other way. Open again. Turn the square so it looks like a diamond and the creases make an X.

3. Now fold the square in half diagonally. Open the fold. Fold the square in half again the other way diagonally. Open.

4. Fold each corner to the center point along the creases.

5. Fold two of the opposite sides to the center, making creases and open them again. Repeat with the other two sides.

6. Open two opposite corners, leaving the other two triangles meeting in the center.

7. Fold the sides to the center over the two unopened triangles. Crease, then let sides stand up again.

8. Hold each side and push your pointer fingers inward on the paper so the pointed end stands up.

T i P

Use your fingernail or side of a pencil to make deeper creases in your paper.

9. Pull out your pointer fingers and fold the end that is standing up, over the top edge, while pressing the sides inward. The point will meet the other triangle points in the bottom of the box. Repeat for the other side.

10. Sharpen your creases to make the box sturdy.

Make one box slightly larger than the other. Slide one over the other for a custom gift box.

You Will Need:

- magazines to cut apart (ask for permission)
- scissors
- card stock
- glue
- pencil
- ruler
- markers, glitter gel pens, regular gel pens, or crayons
- beads, buttons, or other decorations

T i P

Try reusable sticky dots to hold your doll's clothes onto the figure.

Paper dolls were especially popular in Europe in the early 1800s. The dolls and their fancy outfits soon spread to America, where they are still popular today. Make your own paper dolls for fun, and show your designer style.

Here's How:

1. Find a model shown from head to toe in a fashion magazine. Cut out the figure.

2. Trace the figure onto a piece of card stock twice. On one figure's feet, draw a 1 x 3 inch (2.5 x 7.5 centimeter) base. On the other figure, draw small square tabs at each shoulder, arm and at the outside of each leg. Cut out the card stock figures.

3. Glue the magazine cutout to the card stock figure with a base.

4. Snip a 1/2 inch (1.25 centimeter) **vertical** slit in the middle of the card stock base.

5. Measure and cut out a strip of card stock 1 inch x 3 inches (2.5 x 7.5 centimeters)

wide. Snip a 1/2 inch (1.25 centimeter) vertical slit in the center of the strip. Attach the strip to the base by sliding the slit into the slit of the base to make a +. Your doll should now stand up.

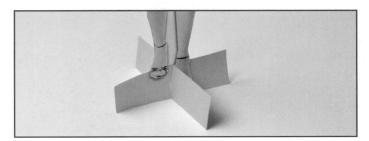

6. Decorate pieces of scrap paper to make your designer fabric. Use the card stock figure with tabs as a template. Trace the template onto the decorated paper for tops and bottoms. Add buttons, jewelry, and other details with markers and gel pens.

7. Cut out your clothes and bend the tabs over your doll for new clothes.

You Will Need:

- small spiral notebook
- colorful scrap paper
- magazines to cut apart (ask for permission)
- scissors
- paper punch
- craft glue
- paper bowl or plastic dish you can throw away
- water
- paintbrush

Confetti Journal Cover

Celebrate your creativity with a **confetti** journal. This idea works on shoe boxes or other forms to make colorful and useful designs.

Here's How:

1. Paper punch, cut, or tear paper into pieces less than 1 inch (2.5 centimeters). Cut pictures and words from magazines. Gather enough to cover your notebook cover.

2. Spread newspaper over your work surface.

3. Squirt enough glue to fill about half of the bottom of the bowl. Dribble a little water into the glue and stir. Add more water until it looks like heavy cream.

4. Paint the glue over the cover. Sprinkle the confetti over the cover. Gently smooth out wrinkles and air bubbles with your fingers. Let it dry.

5. Paint another layer of glue on the cover and sprinkle more confetti, overlapping colors.

6. Place words and pictures where you like them. Again, smooth out the papers and let it dry.

7. Brush another layer of glue over the cover. Let it dry.

8. If you like the effect, repeat the steps on the back cover.

TIP

cut out letters from magazines to spell your name and the word journal, to make a title for your book. For example, your title might be Ellen's Journal.

more Paper crafts

Now that you have some practice with paper crafts, try more difficult projects. Then invent your own! Your creative crafts will make special paper treasures, just as artists made a long time ago.

Glossary

confetti (kuhn-FET-ee): small pieces of colorful paper, usually thrown in celebration at parties, weddings, or parades

knead (NEED): to press, fold, and squish until the material is smooth

origami (or-uh-GAH-mee): the art of folded paper

papier-mâché (PAY-pur muh-SHAY): wet paper soaked in glue that may be molded, before drying into a hard shape

papyrus (puh-PYE-ruhss): a water plant used by ancient Egyptians to make writing paper

piñatas (peen-YAH-tuhz): shapes filled with candy and gifts, which are broken as part of a party game

pulp (PUHLP): a soft, wet mixture

recycled (ree-SYE-kuhld): a new material, such as paper, made from old items

techniques (tek-NEEKS): methods or skills

vertical (VUR-tuh-kuhl): straight up and down

index

Websites to Visit

www.kids.nationalgeographic.com/Activities/Crafts

www.crafts.suite101.com/general

www.easyfunschool.com/

www.home.howstuffworks.com/family-kids-crafts.htm

About The Author

Tracy Nelson Maurer has written more than 60 fiction and nonfiction books for children. She loved crafts as a child and she still likes to take the scissors for a whirl. Tracy lives near Minneapolis, Minnesota, with her husband and two children.